ARCHITECTURAL STYLES YOU CAN IDENTIFY

ARCHITECTURE REFERENCE & SPECIFICATION BOOK

CHILDREN'S ARCHITECTURE BOOKS

BABY PROFESSOR

EDUCATION KIDS

Speedy Publishing LLC

40 E. Main St. #1156

Newark, DE 19711

www.speedypublishing.com

Copyright 2017

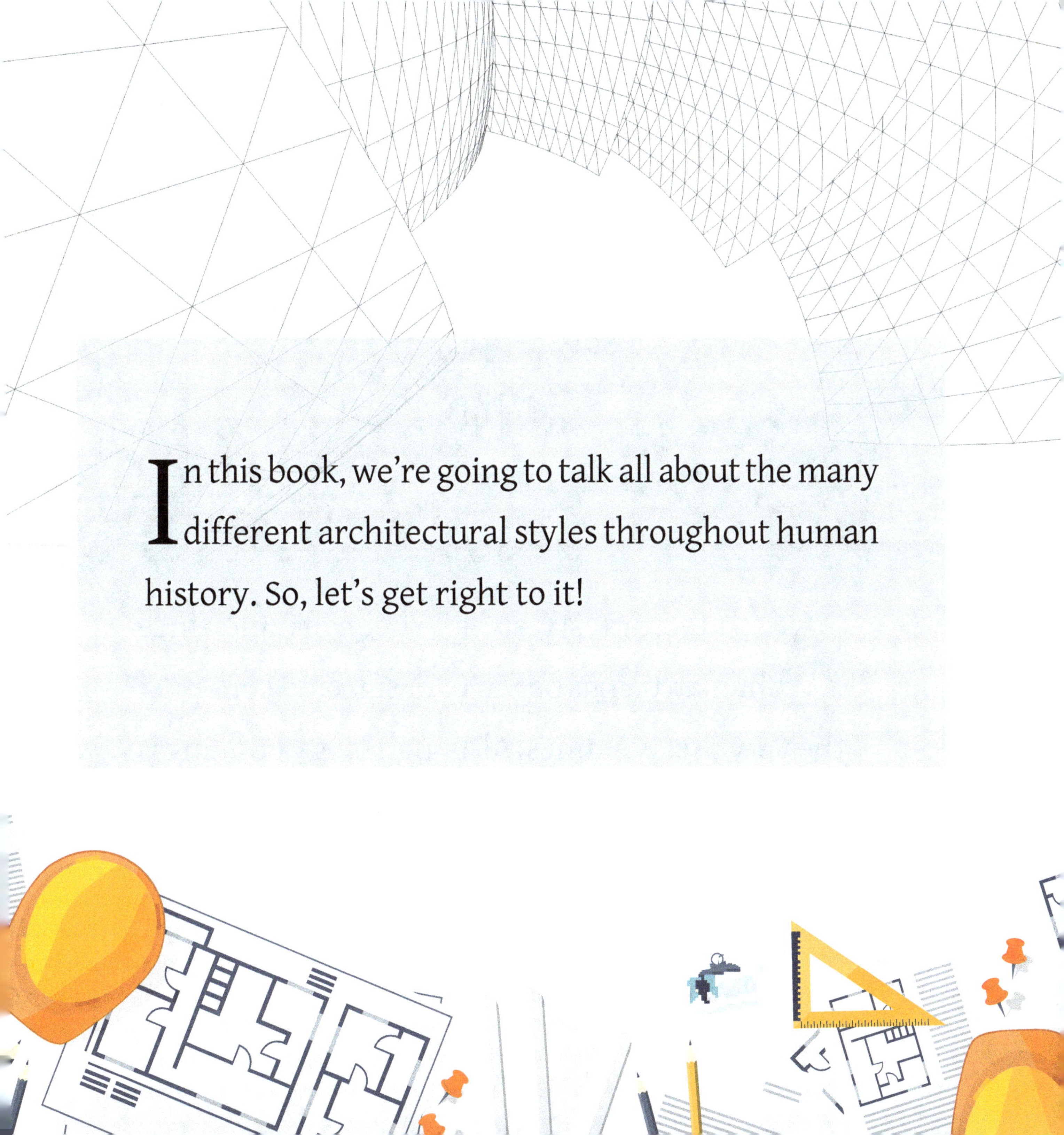

In this book, we're going to talk all about the many different architectural styles throughout human history. So, let's get right to it!

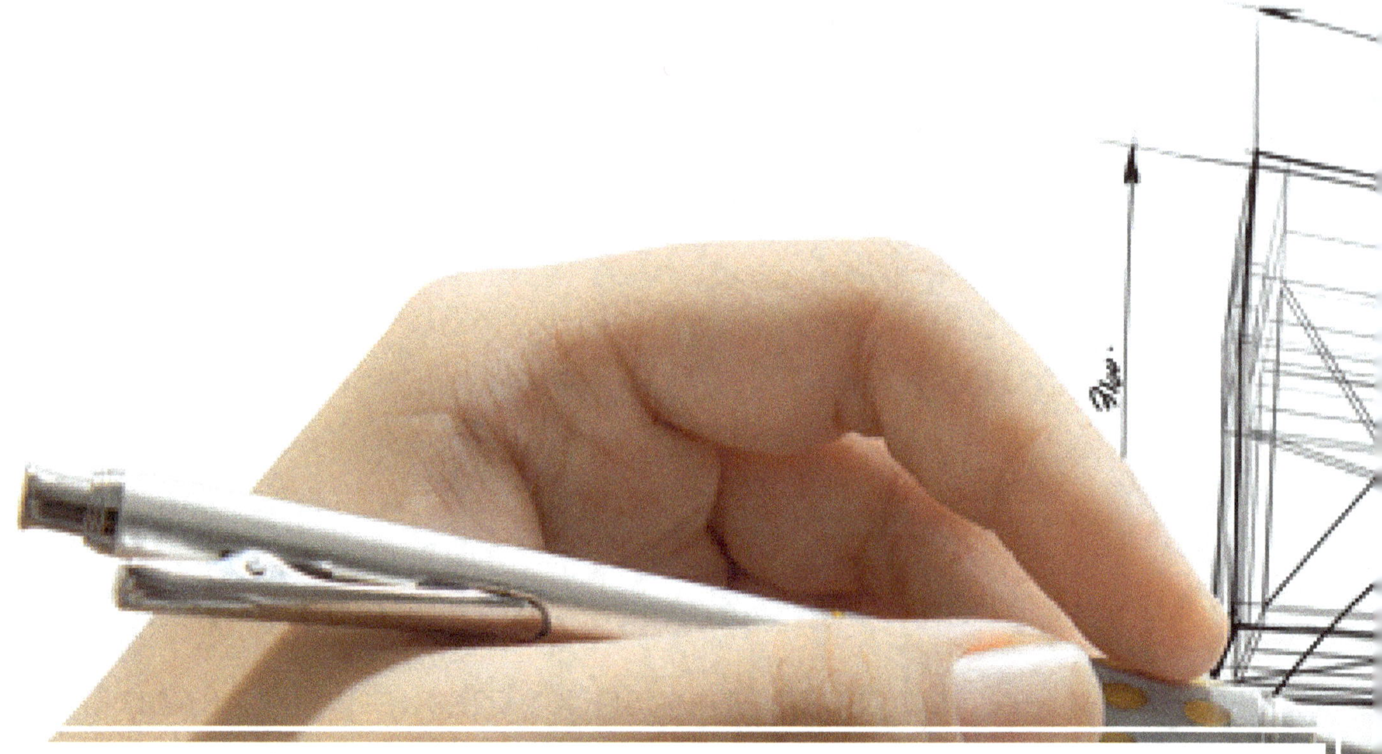

Architectural styles have been around since human beings began to design and construct the very first buildings. Although every building is different, its architectural style can be identified by its design features, age, location, and building materials. As the centuries have passed, each style has influenced the styles that came after it.

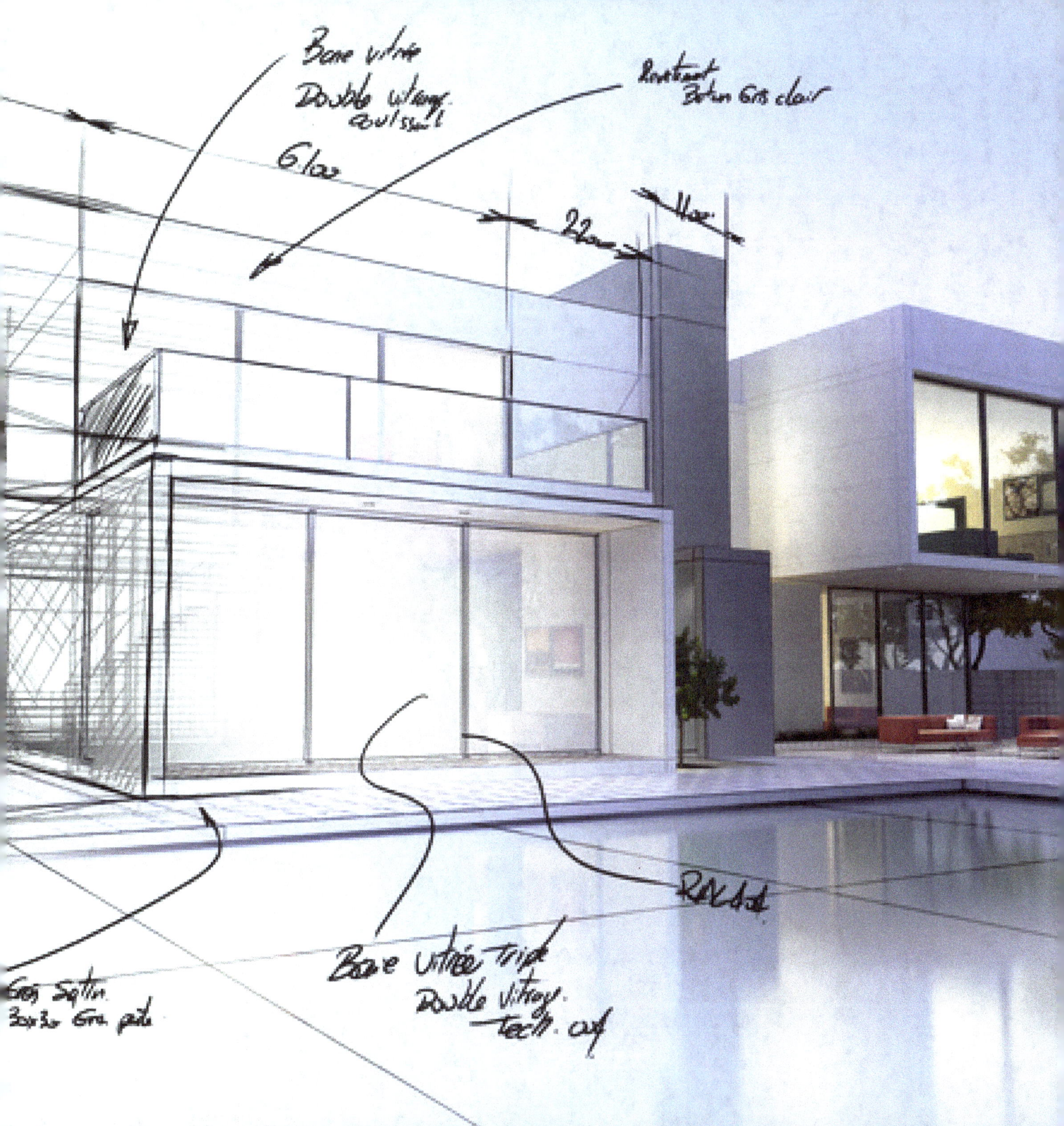

SKARA BRAE, SCOTLAND

NEOLITHIC ARCHITECTURE, CIRCA 10000 BC TO 2000 BC

The Neolithic Age, also called the New Stone Age, was a time when human beings began to make a lot of progress to improve civilization. They developed pottery in addition to tools for hunting and construction.

Neolithic populations in Syria, the northern section of Mesopotamia, and the central region of Asia were proficient builders. They constructed their own dwellings and arranged them in village settlements.

They used bricks made from mud along with plaster and paint. They decorated their dwellings with landscape scenes including animals and people.

GRAND HAR
VICTORIA GATE

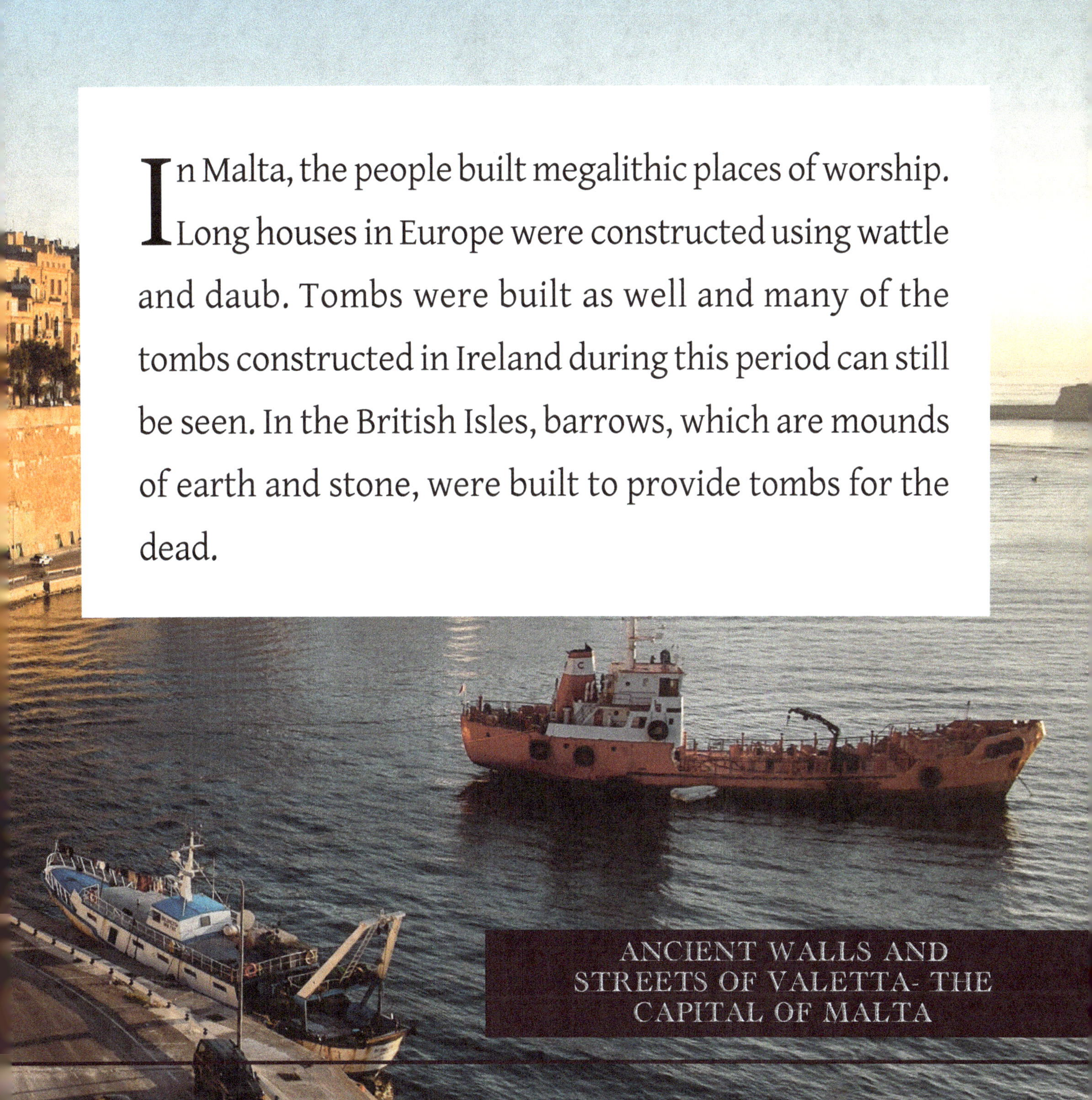

In Malta, the people built megalithic places of worship. Long houses in Europe were constructed using wattle and daub. Tombs were built as well and many of the tombs constructed in Ireland during this period can still be seen. In the British Isles, barrows, which are mounds of earth and stone, were built to provide tombs for the dead.

RING OF BRODGAR, ORKNEY,
SCOTLAND

SUMMARY OF NEOLITHIC ARCHITECTURE

- Made in 10000 to 2000 BC
- Usually one story and were primarily residences, which used mostly horizontal and vertical lines for stability
- Materials used were logs for flooring, clay for sealing the roofs, and wattle and daub, which is a mixture of interwoven twigs solidified with mud

- Located in the Middle East, North Africa, Europe, and the Americas

• Stonehenge in England is a place of worship built
during this time period

ASIAN ARCHITECTURE, CIRCA 5000 BC TO 300 AD

Architecture in Asia developed over many centuries. Characteristics of this style include solid structures made of timber, beautiful stone carvings, and construction using rammed earth, which is a technique for creating walls and floors from highly compressed materials.

BHAGAVAN HALL
DOUGONG

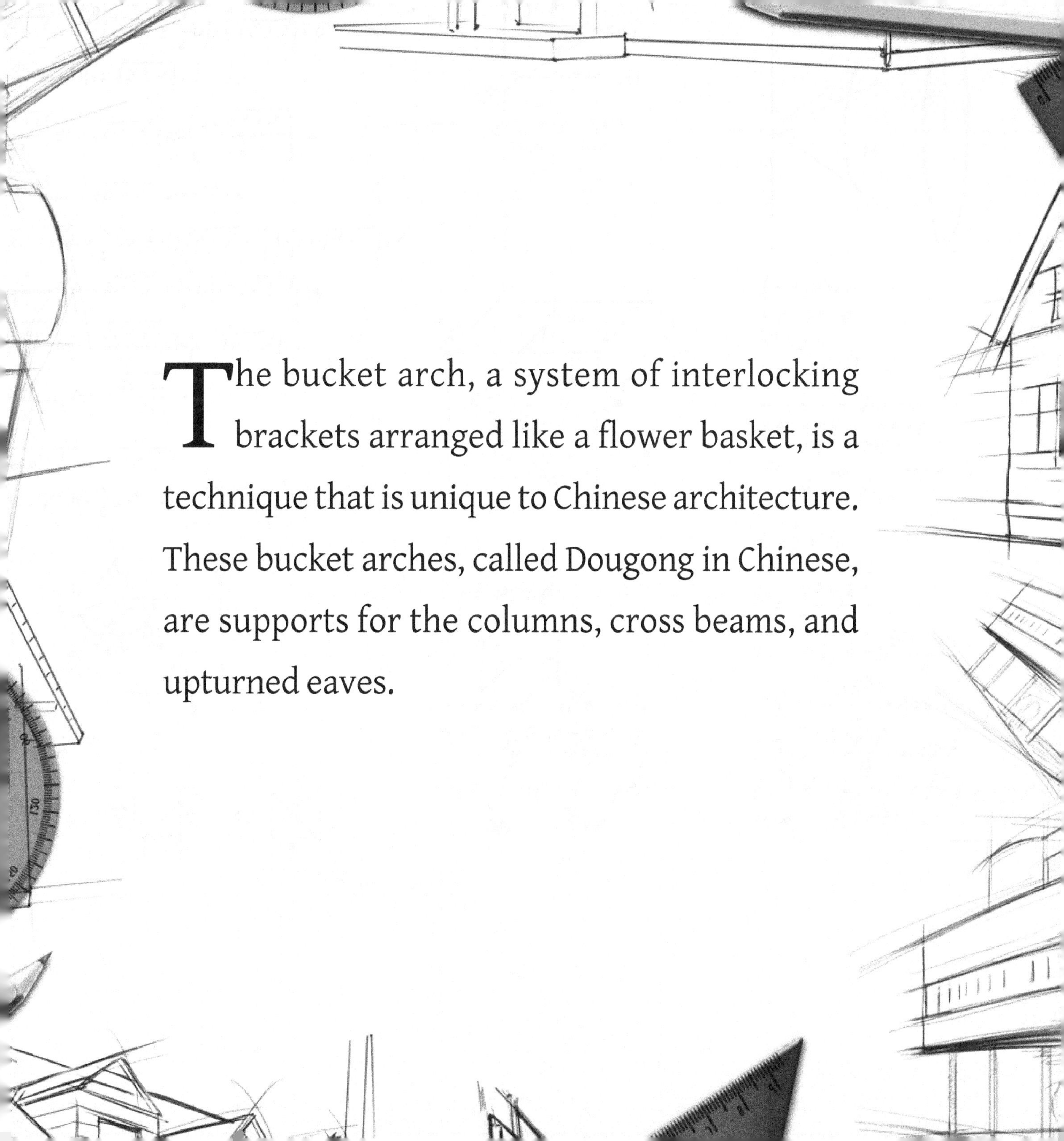

The bucket arch, a system of interlocking brackets arranged like a flower basket, is a technique that is unique to Chinese architecture. These bucket arches, called Dougong in Chinese, are supports for the columns, cross beams, and upturned eaves.

The more important the building was, the more bucket arches there were. Pagodas are another uniquely Asian type of building. They have upturned eaves with tiers on top of each other.

MOUNT FUJI AND
CHUREITO PAGODA

SUMMARY OF ASIAN ARCHITECTURE

- Made in 5000 BC to 300 AD, however, many styles have influenced more modern architecture

- Buildings were designed with a horizontal look, bilateral symmetry, which simply means that when a space is divided in half it looks the same on both sides, and harmonious balance

- Upturned eaves, bucket arches, and tiers are some of the unique features

- Materials used were timber, stone, and rammed earth construction
- Located throughout Asia

- In China, the Great Wall of China, which was begun in the 3rd century BC, and the Forbidden City display the amazing expertise of the architects and construction laborers in past centuries

ANCIENT MEDITERRANEAN ARCHITECTURE, CIRCA 3000 BC TO 300 BC

During this time period, there was much maritime trade. Ancient cultures that lived around the Mediterranean Sea began to exchange design ideas with each other and compete. This was the time period when the Egyptians created their massive stone pyramids and monuments.

ANCIENT
MEDITTERANIAN TEMPLE
RUINS

Around 700 BC, the Greeks began to design enormous columns and transitioned from the Doric style to the Ionic and finally to the Corinthian style, which was the most elaborate of the three.

The Romans adopted much from the style of the Greeks and added the design of arches and an innovative building material that could be shaped when wet but hardened when it dried. It was an early form of concrete.

SUMMARY OF ANCIENT MEDITERRANEAN ARCHITECTURE

- Made in 3000 to 300 Bc
- Elaborate, beautifully designed stone buildings for temples, burial grounds, forums, and private dwellings
- Their interiors were generally more plain than their exteriors
- Materials used were primarily stone and early forms of concrete
- Located in Egypt, Greece, and Rome

- The pyramids in Egypt, the Parthenon in Greece, and the Colosseum in Rome were built during this time period

YUCATAN

Pre-Columbian Architecture, Circa 2000 BC to 1600 AD

This was the era of the great civilizations of Mesoamerica, such as the Mayans and the Aztecs, prior to the arrival of explorers from Europe in 1600 AD, which signaled the beginning of the Colonial period. These different civilizations built amazing stone pyramids with steps topped by temples. They also constructed the first suspension bridges that were built with rope.

SUMMARY OF PRE-COLUMBIAN ARCHITECTURE

- Made in 2000 BC to 1600 AD

- Major buildings were designed as temples, tombs, and monuments

- Materials used were stone, which was cut so perfectly that no mortar was used

- Located primarily in Central America and the Yucatan Peninsula of modern-day Mexico

MAYAN TEMPLE

- Characterized by step pyramids, the largest structures of this type with the exception of ancient Egypt, as well as elaborate roadways

- El Castillo built by the Mayan people is a classic example of this time period

INTERIOR OF SHIEKH ZAYED
MOSQUE, ABUDHABI

ISLAMIC ARCHITECTURE, CIRCA 600 AD TO 1700 AD

The Islamic Empire covered vast distances and this style of architecture, with its beautifully shaped domes and complex archways, was at its peak for over a thousand years. These buildings were intricately designed on the outside and also ornate on the inside.

There were four major types of buildings that were constructed during this time period:

- Mosques for Muslim worshippers
- Palaces for the Islamic rulers

- Tombs for the rulers and their families
- Forts for protection against enemies

DETAILS OF SHEIKH LOTFOLLAH
MOSQUE IN ISFAHAN, IRAN

SUMMARY OF ISLAMIC ARCHITECTURE

- Made in 600 to 1700 AD

- Intricately designed stone buildings for religious mosques, palaces, tombs, and forts as well as public baths, private dwellings, and fountains

- Materials used were primarily stone and precious gems were used for decoration

- Characterized by domes, horseshoe archways, minarets, which are a type of towers, and geometric tile designs

- Located throughout the Islamic Empire, which included sections of Europe, North Africa, the Middle East, India, and sections of China

- The Taj Mahal in India, which is a tomb, and the Dome of the Rock in Jerusalem, which is a mosque, were built during this time period

MEDIEVAL TO RENAISSANCE ARCHITECTURE, CIRCA 500 AD TO 1700 AD

This time period in Europe is described as the Middle Ages and the architectural styles were influence by religion, which was the central core of the culture until the Renaissance brought humanism back to the forefront at the end of this age.

A MEDIEVAL CASTLE OF GUIMARAES'S
CITY IN PORTUGAL.

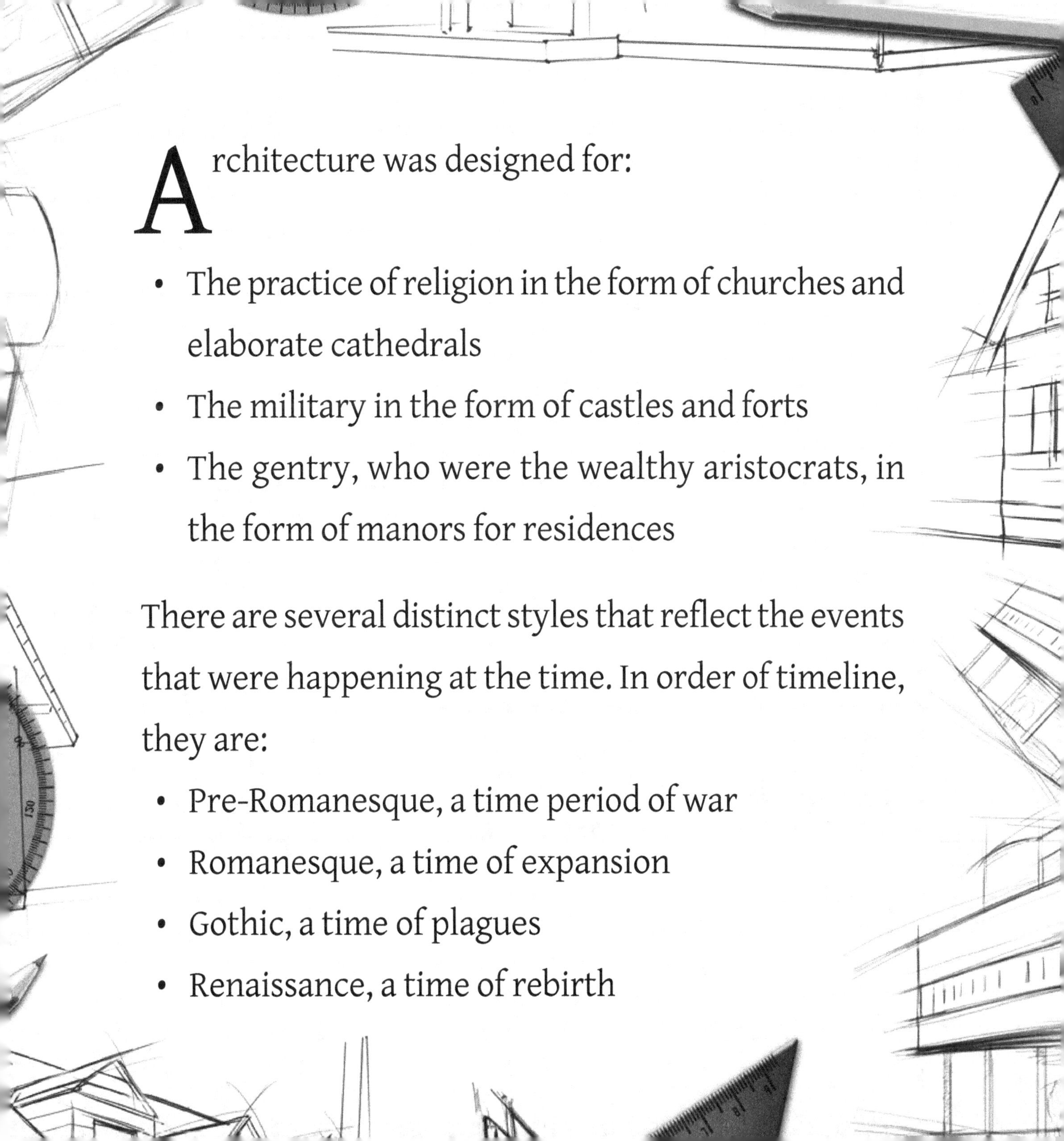

Architecture was designed for:

- The practice of religion in the form of churches and elaborate cathedrals
- The military in the form of castles and forts
- The gentry, who were the wealthy aristocrats, in the form of manors for residences

There are several distinct styles that reflect the events that were happening at the time. In order of timeline, they are:

- Pre-Romanesque, a time period of war
- Romanesque, a time of expansion
- Gothic, a time of plagues
- Renaissance, a time of rebirth

- The Gothic cathedrals of the era were tall stone structures with pointed arches and wall surfaces that were held in place by flying buttresses, which are angled supports from piers on the outside of a building.

This additional support made the high ceilings in Gothic cathedrals possible. They were adorned with sculptures and sometimes gargoyles, which served as water spouts to keep water directed away from the structure.

SUMMARY OF MEDIEVAL TO RENAISSANCE ARCHITECTURE

- Made in 500 to 1700 AD

- Materials used were different types of stone and stained glass

- Characterized by pointed arches, the ribbed vault, which evolved from joint vaulting, simplified walls supported externally by flying buttresses, huge areas of stained glass, and windows in the shape of rosettes

- During the Renaissance there was a revival of ancient Greek and Roman styles including Roman-style columns, arches and domes, and flat ceilings instead of the open ceilings of the Gothic style
- Located throughout Europe

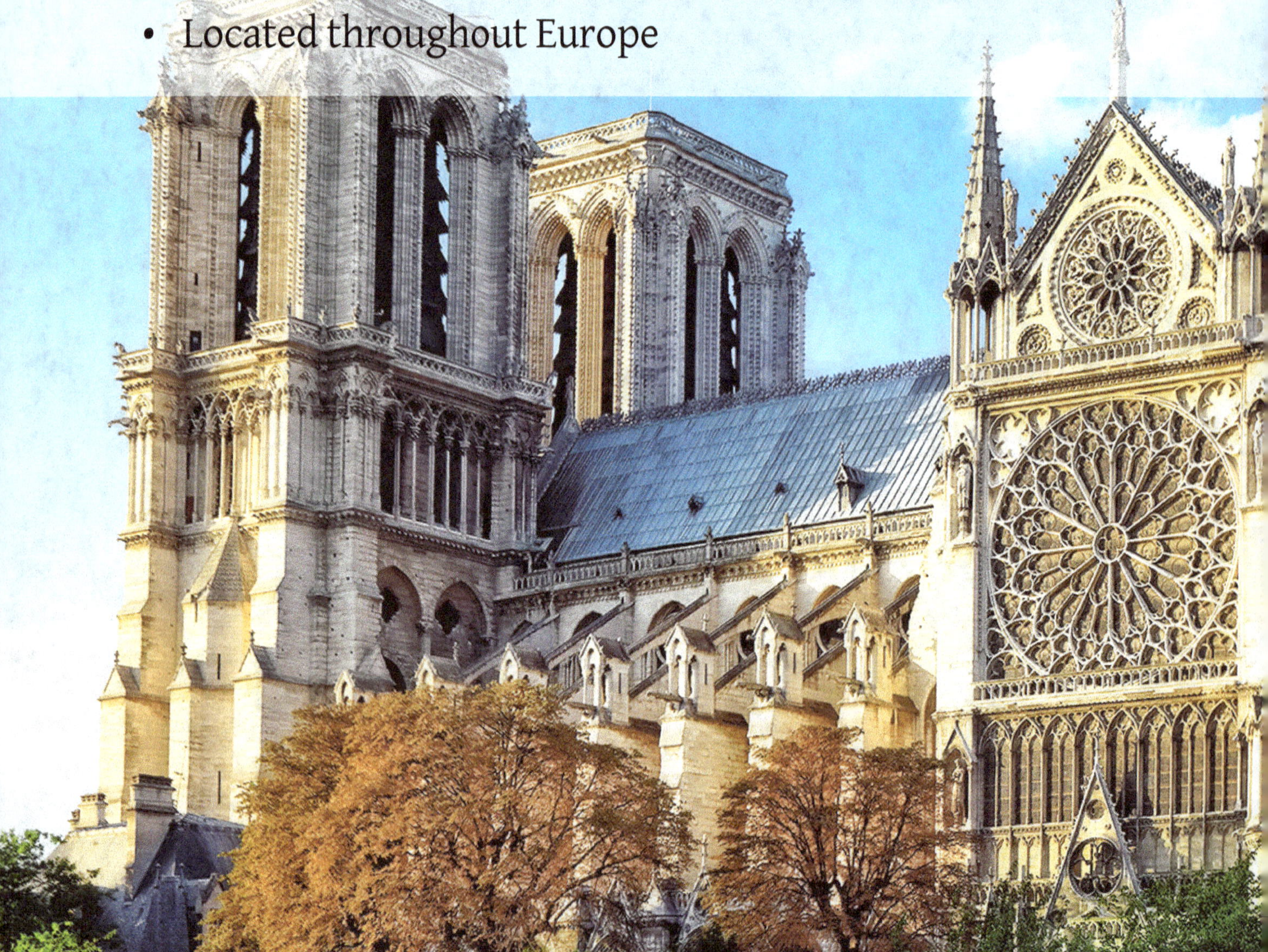

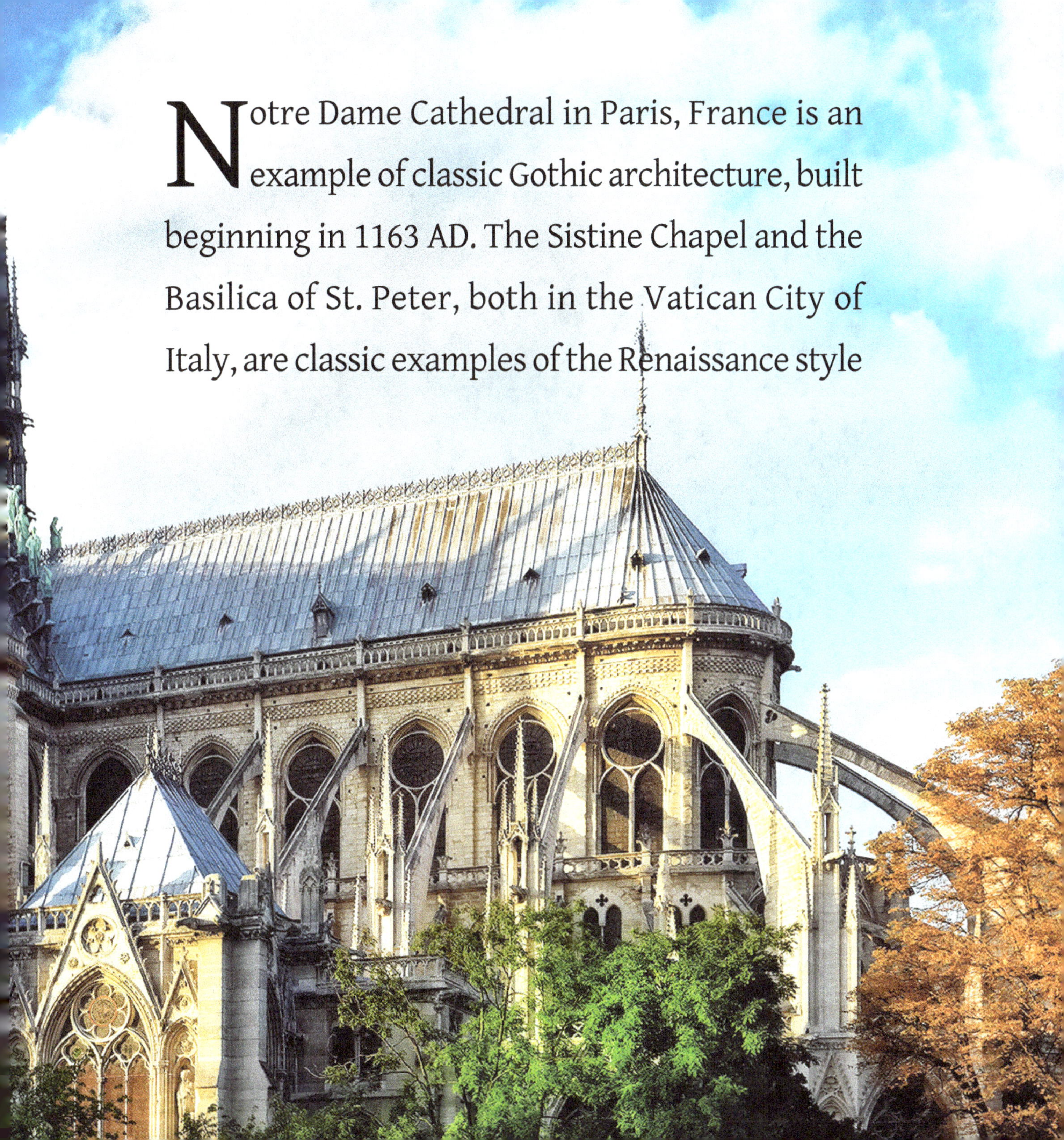
Notre Dame Cathedral in Paris, France is an example of classic Gothic architecture, built beginning in 1163 AD. The Sistine Chapel and the Basilica of St. Peter, both in the Vatican City of Italy, are classic examples of the Renaissance style

SUMMARY

Since ancient times, human beings have wanted their buildings to be beautiful as well as functional. Religion was a driving force behind the development of elaborate architecture. At the beginning, there were temples to gods and goddesses and tombs to ensure that rulers would cross over into the afterlife.

Many of the styles of architecture used in ancient Greece and Rome were used again and again over the centuries. For example, ancient Greek columns were used again by the pagan Romans and revitalized during the Christian era of the Renaissance. This style of column is still in use today in the United States Capitol and other modern buildings.

wesome! Now that you've read about different architectural styles you may want to read about building landmarks in the Baby Professor book Building Landmarks–Bridges, Tunnels and Buildings– Architecture and Design | Children's Engineering Books.

Visit

www.BabyProfessorBooks.com

to download Free Baby Professor eBooks
and view our catalog of new and exciting
Children's Books